WATCH YOUR ENGLISH

WATCH YOUR ENGLISH

COMMON ERRORS IN SPEECH AND WRITING

by

HAROLD HERD

LONDON

GEORGE ALLEN & UNWIN LTD

MUSEUM STREET

First published March 1925
Revised Second Edition 1925
Third Impression (Revised Second Edition) 1926
Fourth Impression (Revised Second Edition) 1929
Fifth Impression (Revised Second Edition) 1932

PRINTED IN GREAT BRITAIN BY
UNWIN BROTHERS LTD., WOKING

PREFACE

THIS is a compact work for the busy man and woman. It lists the commonest faults in speech and writing, and shows the correct forms.

The explanations have been made as simple as possible. Brief definitions of the parts of speech are included for easy reference.

This selection has been guided by observation in my editorial and tutorial work of the errors in the use of English that are constantly being made.

LONDON, 1925.

CONTENTS

WATCH YOUR ENGLISH

THE PARTS OF SPEECH AT A GLANCE

A NOUN is the name of a person or a thing. Examples : John, grass.

A PRONOUN is used instead of a noun. Examples : I, you, she, it, him.

AN ADJECTIVE describes a person or a thing. Examples : A *brave* man. A *beautiful* woman.

A VERB states something about a person or a thing. Examples : He *is* angry. The steamer *leaves* at noon. She *thought* that it was not true. *Has* John *arrived ?*

A PREPOSITION shows the relation between two persons or things. Examples : He knocked *at* the door. There was a book *on* the table.

AN ADVERB qualifies other parts of speech (nouns and pronouns excepted). Usually it tells how a thing was done. Examples : He *slowly* paced the room. The prisoner was *keenly* cross-examined.

A CONJUNCTION connects parts of speech or joins one sentence to another. Examples : You *and* they can settle the difficulty. He was pessimistic about his chances, *but* he won quite easily.

A DICTIONARY OF POPULAR ERRORS

A, An.—An should be used before a vowel, if it has an open sound, and before a silent *h*. A should be used in other cases. Study the following examples :—

> I saw her an hour or two ago. (Silent *h*.)
> He is an honest man. (Silent *h*.)
> It was a unique event. (The *u* is sounded *yoo* ; similarly in eulogy, union, use, etc.)

Accept, Except.—To *accept* means to take what is offered, to answer affirmatively ; to *except* means to leave out or exclude.

> The Corporation accepted the gift with gratitude.
> The invitation was promptly accepted.
> His name was excepted from the list at his express wish.

Adapt, Adopt.—When we *adapt* a thing we make it suitable for our purpose, but if we *adopt* it we imply merely that we have received the thing and embraced it without making any change.

The directors endeavoured in vain to adapt the
   policy to meet present conditions.
Can this equipment be adapted for our purpose ?
The plans were adopted after a short discussion.
The time has come to adopt new methods.

ADJECTIVES FOR ADVERBS.—Frequently an adjective is incorrectly substituted for an adverb.

Correct : The home team pressed *more strongly*
   towards the close of the game.
Incorrect : The home team pressed *stronger* towards
   the close of the game.

ADJECTIVES, POSITION OF.—Be careful to place
the adjective immediately before the noun it
modifies. Sometimes ludicrous errors are made
through neglect of this rule.

Compare, "Stylish Gentlemen's Suits" and
   "Gentlemen's Stylish Suits" (or "Stylish Suits
   for Gentlemen ").

ADVICE, ADVISE.—The confusion of these words
will be avoided if it is borne in mind that *advice* is
a noun, and *advise* a verb.

This advice was generally felt to be sound.
I advise you to return by an early train.

AFFECT, EFFECT.—The verb *affect* means to assume, to imitate, to move, to pretend or to act upon. *To effect* means to cause to be, to accomplish ; used as a noun, *effect* denotes consequence, efficacy, impression, result.

His prospects have been gravely affected.

She was deeply affected.

They affected to regard the decision with indifference.

The transfer was quickly effected.

The effect of this policy has been far-reaching.

The whole effect is admirable.

AGGRAVATE, ANNOY.—To aggravate is to make worse—not to annoy. The following sentences illustrate the correct use of these words :—

It is reported that a wet season has aggravated the conditions.

This report annoyed him.

AGREEMENT OF VERB AND SUBJECT.—(*a*) A noun of multitude (e.g., committee, council) takes the singular verb when it is used collectively. When it is used in a plural sense, however, the verb must also be plural.

The council have adopted the new scheme.

(Say *has adopted*, the council being thought of as a body.)

The committee is at loggerheads on this question.
(In this case the correct verb is *are*, the members
being at loggerheads with one another.)

(*b*) When two singular nouns express practically
the same idea, the singular verb may be used.

His knowledge and experience has been of great
service to the cause.

The second noun is inserted for the sake of
emphasis, and is regarded as part of one idea—
knowledge-and-experience. Similarly, it is permissible to say :—

A cup and saucer is all you need.
This bread and butter is very palatable. (In both
cases a single idea is expressed.)

The following sentences take the plural verb,
because the nouns express distinct ideas.

The personality and record of the leader have
(not *has*) been keenly criticized.
The cup and saucer were (not *was*) broken.

(*c*) The singular verb may be used when the
plural noun is the name of a single thing or unit,
or specifies a quantity.

The United States is (not *are*) competing strongly
in this market.
Ten miles was (not *were*) his average daily walk.

B

(*d*) Certain plural nouns are singular in meaning, and the singular verb should be used.

The news has (not *have*) just been received.
There is (not *are*) no means of ascertaining the
　　exact value.

(*e*) What are known as errors of attraction arise from the verb being made to agree with a noun that comes between the subject and the verb.

The main issue of the elections is (not *are*) now
　　clearly defined.
The causes of this great catastrophe are (not *is*)
　　to be investigated.

(*f*) A plural verb should not be made to do duty also for a singular form occurring in the same predicate, i.e., the part of the sentence that contains the statement.　Note the following correction :—

The chairman said that there were no funds and
　　(*there was*) no likelihood of getting a sufficient
　　response to an appeal for this object.

(*g*) When *as well as* is used instead of *and*, the verb should agree with the first subject.

The captain, as well as his men, *has* endured
　　great hardships.

(*h*) *None* means *not one* and takes the singular verb.

> None of the men is (not *are*) in favour of the proposal.
>
> Is it true that none of our scholars was (not *were*) successful ?

AIN'T.—There is no such word. " It ain't likely " should read : " It is not (or isn't) likely."

ALL RIGHT.—This expression is often erroneously rendered as *alright*, a word that is not to be found in the dictionary.

AND.—As a general rule *and*, which is a conjunction, should not be used to begin a sentence. It is true that well-known authors occasionally employ *and* sentences for the sake of emphasis (as in the following quotation from Arnold Bennett's *Old Wives' Tale*), but the inexperienced writer should be chary of breaking this rule.

> The Square was no longer what it had been, though individual businesses might be as good as ever. For nearly twelve months two shops had been to let in it. And once, bankruptcy had stained its annals.

AND WHICH.—It is permissible to insert *and* before *which* only when the same noun is antecedent, i.e., has been used in the preceding part of the sentence.

Correct : He founded a business which grew
rapidly, and which is still prospering after
twenty-five years.

Incorrect : He founded a business in the High
Street, and which grew rapidly.

ANTE, ANTI.—*Ante* means before, as in ante-
chamber and antediluvian. *Anti* means against,
opposite. Examples : Anti-war, anti-climax.

ANXIETY, DESIRE.—Frequently the word *anxious*
is used when no anxiety is felt. For example, do
not say "I am anxious to get a copy," when you
simply mean "I desire to get a copy."

ANY, EITHER.—*Either* should be used for two
things ; *any* when referring to more than two.

Either of these three policies should meet the
need.   (Substitute *any one*.)

APT, LIKELY.—*Apt* implies fitness, inclination or
suitability, and should not be employed in the sense
of probability.

He is likely (not *apt*) to miss the boat.

ARTIST, ARTISTE.—*Artiste* is the feminine form of
the word artist, which we have borrowed from the
French. According to English usage, however, an
artist is a painter, or anyone who practises a fine
art ; an *artiste* is a professional singer, pianist,
violinist, dancer, etc.—irrespective of sex.

As, Like.—Care should be taken not to use *like* instead of *as*. Say, "You must do as (not *like*) he does."

As, That.—The use of *as* for *that* should be avoided.

He did not say that (not *as*) you would be here to-day.

As per.—This phrase has been overworked in commercial letters, and should in any case be avoided as an ugly construction. It should never be used in personal letters, e.g., "I saw him yesterday as per your suggestion." Write instead, "I saw him yesterday, as you suggested."

Averse.—Say "averse to," not "averse from."

Belongs to.—This phrase means is owned by. You may say, "This motor-car belongs to me," but not "I belong to (i.e., I am owned by) this motor-car."

Beside, Besides.—*Beside* means by, close to ; *besides*, in addition to, moreover.

I first saw him beside the main entrance.

Have you any money besides this ?

Besides, the season will not be over for at least a month.

Between, Among, Amongst.—*Between* refers to two persons or things ; *among* or *amongst* to more than two.

The work was divided between the two men.

She distributed the sweets among the six children.

Between is used for more than two when it expresses the meaning more definitely than *among*. Example :—

A truce has been arranged between the three parties.

Between should not be used with *each*. Say, " There was an interval of five minutes between the bombardments " (not " between each bombardment ").

CAN, MAY.—The distinction between these words is that the former denotes ability, and the latter implies permission or possibility. In the following sentence, which illustrates the most common form of mistake, substitute *may* for *can* :—

Can I call to see you to-morrow ?

CANVAS, CANVASS.—*Canvas* is a strong coarse cloth. To *canvass* is to examine, discuss, solicit.

CAST, CASTE.—The list of actors taking part in a play is known as the *cast*. *Caste* denotes an exclusive class.

COLLUSION, CO-OPERATION.—*Collusion* implies a secret understanding for a wrong purpose ; *co-operation* means acting together. The following examples show the distinction :—

The judge said that he suspected collusion between the parties in this case.

The excellent results of the past year's working were mainly due to the hearty co-operation of employers and employed.

COMPLACENT, COMPLAISANT.—*Complacent* means pleased, satisfied; *complaisant* means obliging, polite, eager to please.

His complacent expression told them that he had won the day.
They were received by a complaisant secretary.

COMPLEMENT, COMPLIMENT.—The full number or quantity, or that which completes it, is called the *complement*. Distinguish this word from *compliment*, which means an expression of praise.

These recruits bring us up to our complement.
No higher compliment has ever been paid to the town.

CONFIDANT, CONFIDENT.—A person who is entrusted with secrets is a *confidant* (feminine, *confidante*). *Confident* means to be bold, trusting, fully assured.

CONSIDER.—This word is sometimes incorrectly used instead of *think* or *believe*. Its meaning is to contemplate, to reflect.

Correct : The matter has been fully considered.
Incorrect : I consider you are wrong. (Say *think*.)

CONTINUAL, CONTINUOUS.—*Continual* means very frequent ; *continuous* means uninterrupted.

There have been continual breaches of the bye-laws.

The noise of battle was continuous.

COUNCIL, COUNSEL.—A *council* is any deliberative body, e.g., London County Council. *Counsel* means advice, and to counsel is to advise.

CREDIBLE, CREDITABLE, CREDULOUS.—*Credible* means worthy of belief ; *creditable*, worthy of credit or praise ; *credulous*, showing undue readiness to believe.

This statement is not credible.

His performance was generally regarded as creditable.

He has suffered the penalty of being credulous.

DEFINITE, DEFINITIVE.—*Definite* implies that a thing is precise ; *definitive* means that it is final.

The terms are definite.

This verdict is definitive

DEPRECATE, DEPRECIATE.—To *deprecate* is to protest against, to express disapproval of ; *depreciate* means to lower in price, to belittle.

He deprecated hasty action in this matter.

Prices have rapidly depreciated.

His object was to depreciate our efforts.

DIFFERENT.—Say " different from," not " different to."

DON'T, DOESN'T.—*Don't* is a contraction of *do not* and should be used only in connection with plural nouns and pronouns ; *doesn't* is a conversational form of *does not*, and should be employed only in connection with singular nouns and pronouns.

> *Correct :* He doesn't think that you have a chance.
> *Incorrect :* They doesn't know the cause of the delay.   (Say *don't*.)

DOUBLE NEGATIVE.—A sentence that contains two negatives is rendered affirmative.   It is incorrect to say " I haven't done nothing," and does not express the intended meaning, which is " I haven't done anything " or " I have done nothing."

EACH, EVERY, EVERYONE.—The singular pronoun should be used.

> Each watched keenly for *his* cue.
> Every boy will be given *his* chance.
> Everyone must do *his* duty.

The masculine pronoun should be used if two genders are implied.

> Every clerk must be at *his* desk at 9 a.m.

Both pronouns may be used when it is desired to specify both sexes.

EITHER, OR; NEITHER, NOR.—*Either* takes *or*, *neither* takes *nor*.

You can return either by 'bus *or* train.
Neither time *nor* trouble will be spared.

Either means one or the other; *neither* means not either. The words cannot be used with reference to more than two persons or things. Both take the singular verb.

Either Grey or Smith is (not *are*) responsible.
Neither the manager nor his assistant is (not *are*) at the office.

FARTHER, FURTHER.—*Farther* implies distance; *further* means also, besides, moreover, in addition.

The explorers decided that it would be dangerous to go any farther.
A further statement has been issued.
Further, we have evidence to show . . .

It will be observed, nevertheless, that many well-known writers do not make this distinction.

FOREGO, FORGO.—To *forego* means to precede in place or time; to *forgo* is to abstain from, go without, relinquish.

The foregoing facts must be borne in mind.
Is it really a foregone conclusion ?

He decided to forgo this pleasure.

It was not thought that they would forgo the opportunity.

FORMALLY, FORMERLY.—*Formally* means in accordance with the usual forms, ceremony, or conventions ; *formerly* denotes at an earlier period.

Mr. Brown was formally elected this morning.

Do you know that they were formerly neighbours of ours ?

FORMER, LATTER ; FIRST, LAST.—*Former* and *latter* mean respectively the first-mentioned and second-mentioned of two persons or things. If you wish to refer to more than two, substitute first, first-named, or first-mentioned ; last, last-named, or last-mentioned.

GOT.—This word should be employed only when obtained is meant. It is incorrect to say, " The child has got appealing ways."

HANGED, HUNG.—*Hanged* refers only to capital punishment ; *hung* applies to things.

The two murderers were hanged this morning.

She hung the pictures on the wall.

HAS A RIGHT TO, OUGHT TO.—We may say of a man that " He ought to be punished," but not that " He has a right to be punished."

IN, INTO.—*In* denotes within ; *into* implies motion from the outside to the inside. The distinction will be more readily grasped after studying the following examples :—

He is waiting in the office.
He walked into the office.
They were in the garden a minute ago.
They went into the garden a few minutes ago.

IN (UNDER) THE CIRCUMSTANCES.—Say " In the circumstances," not " Under the circumstances."

INDICT, INDITE.—To *indict* means to accuse ; to *indite* is to compose, to write.

The man will not be indicted on this evidence. (*Note.*—In the strict legal sense, to indict is to charge a person by finding of a grand jury, which conducts a preliminary review of the evidence and determines whether it is sufficient to justify a trial.)

He indited a short letter.

INDIVIDUAL.—This word is frequently misused. *Individual* means single or particular as opposed to general. An *individual* is a member of a class, community, etc. The word should not be employed as meaning person.

Every man thinks that his experience is individual.

The rights of the community must come before the convenience of the individual.

INGENIOUS, INGENUOUS.—*Ingenious* means clever, skilful ; *ingenuous*—open, frank, artless.

INVITE.—This is a verb and cannot be used as a noun. Write " Many thanks for your invitation " (not *invite*).

ITS, IT'S.—The former is the possessive form of the pronoun *it*, and does not take the apostrophe ; the latter is a contraction of *it is*, and always requires the apostrophe.

The child was playing with its toys.
" It's the third time I have missed this train," he panted.

JUDICIAL, JUDICIOUS.—*Judicial* means pertaining to a court of law, impartial ; *judicious* means prudent, of sound judgment.

The judicial hearing began yesterday.
His conduct throughout was most judicious.

LAY, LIE.—Errors in the use of these words are common, and have occasionally crept into the work of great writers. *Lay* is usually transitive, which means that it has a direct object ; *lie* is intransitive, i.e., it does not take a direct object, the action being confined to the persons mentioned.

Lay.

Lay the book (object) on the table.

She was laying the table (object).

He laid the book (object) on the table.

They have laid the book (object) on the table.

Lay is also used reflexively, which means that it acts upon the person mentioned.

He laid himself on the couch.

Lie.

Lie down!

She lies down.

The book is lying on the table.

The past tense is *lay :—*

She lay down.

The book lay on the table.

The past participle is *lain :—*

She has lain down.

The book has lain on the table for some days.

Note that in all these cases the action is *limited to the person or thing.*

LEARN, TEACH.—To *learn* means to obtain knowledge or receive instruction ; to *teach* is to give instruction.

I am told that they teach (not *learn*) you book-keeping in one month.

LIBEL, SLANDER.—These words are frequently confused. The simple distinction is that libel is written or printed, but slander is spoken.

LOOSE, LOSE.—The former word denotes slack, relaxed, vague, and to unbind or set free; the latter means to cease to possess. Study these examples :—

The knot was loosely tied.

The loose wording of the Act will give rise to endless litigation.

It is foolish to carry so much loose money.

He was determined not to lose this opportunity.

You will lose those papers if you leave them lying about.

LUXURIANT, LUXURIOUS.—*Luxuriant* means abundant or exuberant; *luxurious* denotes given to luxury.

What is the explanation of this luxuriant growth?

His tastes are too luxurious for his position.

MUTUAL.—This word is frequently misused. The best known error is in the title of Charles Dickens's novel, *Our Mutual Friend*. Mutual means a relation between two or more persons or things, and implies that they are *equally concerned in the action or feeling*. It is correctly used in the following sentences :—

Mutual understanding has smoothed their path in life.

They had a mutual dislike.

It would be unnecessary repetition to say, " They had a mutual dislike for each other," the words each other being implied by *mutual*.

Me Having, My Having.—Say " Will you acknowledge my having paid this money ? " not " Will you acknowledge me having paid this money ? "

Myself, Yourself, etc.—Avoid the incorrect use of these and similar pronouns.

My partner and I (not *myself*) will deal with the matter this morning.

He addressed it to you (not *yourself*).

The legitimate use of these pronouns (which are emphatic and reflexive) is illustrated in the following sentences :—

I have examined the original document myself (or I myself have, etc.).

You signed the letter yourself (or You yourself, etc.).

None.—See Agreement of Subject and Verb (*h*).

Observance, Observation.—*Observance* means a duty, rite, custom, or the performance of a duty, etc. ; *observation* means watching, taking notice.

This interesting observance dates back over three hundred years.

His narrative reveals unusual powers of observation.

OFFICIAL, OFFICIOUS.—*Official* means authoritative, or pertaining to office ; *officious* denotes intrusive or meddlesome.

The news is official.
I have received official help in the matter.
His officious action was keenly resented.

ONE.—The rule for the impersonal use of *one* is simply that you must employ it throughout. It is not permissible to begin with *one* and then use *his* and *he*.

Correct : One must keep fit if one wishes to enjoy oneself.

Incorrect : One must keep his enthusiasm alive if he is to become an expert player. (One must keep one's enthusiasm alive if one, etc.)

ONLY, PLACING OF.—The adverb *only* should be inserted close to the word it modifies. The careless placing of this adverb frequently results in absurdity or ambiguity. " He had only made one mistake " implies that he had made nothing else. The correct form is " . . . made only one mistake."

How the meaning of a sentence is affected by the placing of *only* is illustrated by the following constructions :—

I saw them only yesterday.
I saw only them yesterday.
I only saw them yesterday.

The literal meaning of the last example is " I saw them but did not speak to them yesterday."

PARTIALLY, PARTLY.—When you wish to convey that a thing is not complete, use *partly* if possible. *Partially* has the primary meaning of biased, unfair. Observe the double meaning of the word in this sentence : " The appeal was partially heard before the Lord Chief Justice, Mr. Justice —— and Mr. Justice —— yesterday."

PARTY.—A *party* is a body of persons, and it is therefore incorrect to use the word instead of person. Legally, a *party* denotes each side (one or more persons) in an action or a contract. In the following sentence substitute man or woman :—

They were amused at the sight of an elderly party running to catch the train.

PER.—This word is commonly used in commercial correspondence, but should be avoided in articles, personal letters, etc.

The delegates are leaving by (not *per*) aeroplane to-morrow.

PERSONALITY, PERSONALTY.—*Personality* means personal existence, a distinctive personal character ; *personalty* denotes personal estate

PHASE, PHRASE.—A *phase* is an aspect of a moon or a planet, or any state of change or development ;

a *phrase* is a short expression, a small group of words, or a mode of expression.

PRACTICAL, PRACTICABLE.—That which can be done is *practicable* ; that which is based on practice or experience is said to be *practical*.

His suggestions were practical.

I am sorry that the plan is not practicable, as it would involve a much larger outlay than the directors would sanction.

PRACTICE, PRACTISE.—The former word is a noun and the latter a verb.

You will find this practice most helpful.

I advise you to practise this exercise daily.

PRECEDENT, PRECEDENCE.—A *precedent* is a previous parallel case, e.g., a legal judgment or a line of political action that serves as an example in subsequent cases. *Precedence* means going before, superiority.

Correct : Is there a precedent for this step ?

He is entitled to take precedence.

Incorrect : It is the clear duty of Mr. —— to resign at once in accordance with precedence. (Substitute precedent.)

PREPOSITION AT END OF SENTENCE.—It is not good style to end a sentence with a preposition, which is too weak for an emphatic position.

Correct : This is the policy *to* which we are committed.

Incorrect : This is the policy we are committed *to*.

Though prepositional endings are generally to be avoided, exceptions are occasionally desirable to escape an awkward construction.

It is permissible to use a prepositional verb (i.e., a verb and preposition which form a compound) at the end of a sentence.

They complained of being *stared at*.

PRINCIPAL, PRINCIPLE.—*Principal* means the highest in rank, grade or importance, chief, main, leading. A *principle* is a law or rule of action.

What are the principal measures to be taken ?
The principle of the new scheme won unanimous support.
He is a man without principle.

PRONOUNS, CASE OF.—When two pronouns are joined by *and*, the wrong case is frequently used for the second pronoun. Both must have the same case. If they are the subject of a sentence, use the nominative case ; if they are the object or are governed by a preposition (e.g., between), use the objective case.

Correct :

You and I can deal with the matter.

He and we must decide.

They will call for her and me.

Between you and me.

Incorrect :

You and me can deal with the matter.

He and us must decide.

They will call for her and I.

Between you and I.

The wrong pronoun is commonly used after *let.* Say "Let you and me," not "Let you and I." The pronoun is the object of *let.*

Say "It is I" not "It is me," the correct case after any part of the verb *to be* (are, was, were, etc.) being the nominative.

If it were she (not *her*) who did it.

The case after *as* and *than* is another common source of error. The rule is that they must have the same verb after as before, and the correctness of a sentence can be tested by adding the implied words.

I envy you more than her.

(Right if it means "I envy you more than I envy her"; wrong if the meaning is "I envy you more than she does.")

I am as good a shot as him.

(Wrong, because we cannot say *him is.*)

PRONOUNS, PRECEDENCE OF.—The order of pronouns is governed by these rules : (*a*) Put first the pronoun of the person addressed ; (*b*) follow with the pronouns of the persons mentioned ; (*c*) place last the pronoun indicating the speaker.

You, Brown, and I can settle this matter.
Smith and I are going to the theatre to-night.

RAISE, RISE.—It is correct to say that a man has been given a *rise* (i.e., an increase of wages)—not a *raise*.

RESPECTFULLY, RESPECTIVELY.—*Respectfully* implies with respect ; *respectively* means severally or proper to each. Say " Yours respectfully," not " Yours respectively."

SAME, SIMILAR.—The former word denotes identity ; the latter implies mere likeness.

He was positive that it was the same man.
It is a house of similar design to ours.
" Your order to hand and same is receiving attention." This use of *same* should be avoided. Write instead : " Thank you for your order, which is receiving attention."

SHALL, SHOULD ; WILL, WOULD.—The confusion of *shall* and *will* is one of the commonest errors in speaking and writing English. The following should be carefully studied :—

Simple Future.

I shall read.	We shall read.
Thou wilt read.	You will read.
He will read.	They will read.

Command, Intention, Determination or Promise.

I will read.	We will read.
Thou shalt read.	You shall read.
He shall read.	They shall read.

When the future action, etc., is contingent, the following forms should be used :—

I should read.	We should read.
Thou wouldst read.	You would read.
He would read.	They would read.

When you desire also to express promise, determination, obligation, etc., the following are the correct forms :—

I would read.	We would read.
Thou shouldst read.	You should read.
He should read.	They should read.

The way to avoid confusion between *shall* and *will* and *should* and *would* is to be sure of the meaning that you wish to convey. " I will complete five years' service to-morrow " is wrong, because simple futurity is implied by the completion of the term— not determination. Following are a few examples :—

I shall (not *will*) be pleased to hear from you.

I should (not *would*) not be ready in time.

We shall (not *will*) be at home next week.

We should (not *would*) be grateful for an early decision.

When asking a second-person question, the employment of *shall* or *will* is determined by the answer expected For example :—

Shall you be at home to-morrow ?   (Yes, I shall.)

Will you do it ?   (Yes, I will.)

SHEW, SHOW.—The latter is the modern form of the verb, and should invariably be used.

SKILFUL, SKILLED.—Both words imply the possession or display of skill, but the best usage limits *skilled* to labour, e.g., a skilled artificer.

SPLIT INFINITIVE.—The insertion of a word or words between *to* (which marks the infinitive) and the verb is termed splitting the infinitive.

Correct :

To wander freely (or Freely *to wander*).

To assume immediately (or Immediately *to assume*).

Incorrect :

To freely *wander*.

To immediately *assume*.

STATIONARY, STATIONERY.—*Stationary* means fixed, not moving ; *stationery* is a general term for writing materials.

STATUE, STATUTE.—A *statue* is an image of a person or an animal ; a *statute* is a law.

SUPERLATIVE DEGREE.—Use the superlative degree only when referring to three or more things. When two things are compared, employ the comparative degree.

Which is the *better* of these two ?

There were 36 entries, but the judges had no difficulty in deciding that Mr. Brown's exhibit was the *best*.

TASTEFULLY, TASTILY.—A thing that shows taste may be said to be *tastefully* done. *Tastily* is a vulgarism.

THAT.—This word should not be used as an adverb.

He was surprised to find the well so (not *that*) deep.

THAT, WHICH, WHO.—Modern usage favours *that* instead of *which* in a defining clause, i.e., a part of a sentence that specifies the scope of the preceding noun. The following examples show the correct use of *that* and *which* :—

Defining : Where is the book that I gave you ?

Non-defining : The book, which is now in its tenth edition, was first issued in January.

Defining : This is the policy that will conquer.

Non-defining : This policy, which is unanimously supported by the leaders, will conquer.

" That . . . that " is not permissible.

That is the book which (not *that*) I gave you.

Who is preferable for persons.

The man who (not *that*) wins promotion.

THE SAID.—This phrase should not be used except in legal documents. " I hear that a new candidate has been chosen to contest your division. Do you know the said candidate ? " How much simpler to write *him* instead of *the said candidate !*

THEIR, THERE.—The former word means of, or belonging to them ; the latter denotes that place.

They are spending their holiday at Scarborough.
I was there a fortnight ago.
Can you give me their address ?
There it is—on that post card.

THEM, THESE, THOSE.—*Them* is the objective form of *they* and cannot be used instead of *these* (plural of *this*) and *those* (plural of *that*).

Pass me those (not *them*) things.
Are these (not *them*) your dogs ?

THIS KIND, THAT KIND.—It is incorrect to say *these kind* or *those kind*, because the noun is singular. The correct forms are *this kind* and *that kind*. We may, however, say *these kinds* and *those kinds*, because the nouns are plural.

To, Omission of.—It is not good English to say "I wrote him yesterday." "I wrote to him yesterday" is the correct form.

To, Too, Two.—These words are sometimes confused. *To* indicates motion towards, and is the sign of the infinitive (e.g., to read, to walk); *too* denotes also, more than enough; *two* means twice one.

Transpire.—*Transpire* means to exhale, to ooze out, to become known. It should not be used instead of *happen*.

"Try and——"—It is incorrect to say "Try and finish the work to-day." Substitute *to* for *and* in this and similar sentences. (As the sentence stands it means "Try and you must finish the work to-day.")

Unattached Participle.—When you use a participle see that it is attached to a noun or a pronoun.

Correct : As I was *opening* the door, a dog attacked me.

Incorrect : Opening the door, a dog attacked me.

Correct : As he was *crossing* the street, a motor-car ran over him.

Incorrect : Crossing the street, a motor-car ran over him.

Unique.—This word denotes the only one of its kind, and cannot be qualified. It is therefore incorrect to describe anything as "strikingly unique."

Very.—We may write "It was very annoying," but not "I am very annoyed." The correct form is " I am much (or greatly) annoyed." Similarly, " I am much interested " (troubled, surprised, etc.).

WAS, WERE.—The subjunctive use of *were* perplexes many writers. This question serves as a test : " Is the sentence conditional ? " If there is no element of doubt, use *was*.

> An inquiry was made ten years ago to determine whether this were practicable. (Substitute *was*, because no condition is now implied.)
>
> If it was correct the Government would take action. (This should read " If it were correct, etc.," a condition being implied.)

WHILE.—This word should not be used instead of *and*.

> They bought three books, and (not *while*) John bought a newspaper.

It is permissible to use *while* in making a contrast, when it has the meaning of although.

> While it is literally true, you must admit that it is false in spirit.

WHO, WHOM.—*Who* is used when it is the subject of a sentence ; *whom* is used in the objective case.

> Whom (not *who*) have you asked ? (*Whom* is the object of asked.)

It was she who (not *whom*) I saw clearly would
be blamed.

(The insertion of commas before and after "I
saw clearly" makes it evident that "she *whom* would
be blamed" is incorrect.)

WRONG TENSE.—The sentence "I should have
liked to have been present" typifies a common error.
As it stands the meaning is "I should have liked on
that occasion to be present on a previous occasion."
Substitute *to be* for *to have been*. The rule is that
the present tense must be used when past time has
been indicated by the first verb.

YOURS.—This is the possessive form of the pronoun *your*, and does not take the apostrophe.

SAY WHAT YOU MEAN!

Much inconvenience and misunderstanding would be avoided if everyone who wrote made a conscientious effort to express his meaning plainly. A few illustrations are given below of clumsy or obscure sentences, and in every case an improved construction is suggested.

I am still a councillor but will shortly retire, although I can never hope to be disinterested in public questions.

(I intend to retire shortly from the Council, although I hope never to lose my interest in public questions.)

He arrived on a bicycle breathless and splashed from head to toe.

(He was breathless and splashed from head to toe when he arrived on a bicycle.)

The new road runs down to the river, and it is very deep.

(The new road runs down to the river, which is very deep.)

The man was dressed in grey that arrived yesterday.

(The man who arrived yesterday was dressed in grey.)

Many thanks for your offer, which I shall be pleased to accept.

(Many thanks for your offer, which I have pleasure in accepting.)

His work is superior to an experienced craftsman.

(His work is superior to that of an experienced craftsman.)

This costume suits her better than Mary.

(This costume suits her better than it suits Mary.)

Advertisement in a shop window: Leave your deposit now. It may be gone when you come back.

(Leave your deposit now, otherwise the clock may be gone when you come back.)

WASTED WORDS

NEEDLESS repetition of an idea is a common fault in writing. The superfluous words in the following examples are denoted by italics :—

He ascended *up* the stairs.

She repeated the *same* statement.

It was made of *black* ebony.

The man was an *aged* octogenarian.

You can decide *as to* whether this should be done.

We shall finish *up* the job at the end of this *present* month.

It is one of the finest shops in *the city of* Birmingham.

They crossed the road *to the other side*.

Let us *make up our minds and* determine not to spare any effort to defeat this plan.

AVOID AFFECTATION

SIMPLICITY is the leading characteristic of modern literary style. The man who writes good English avoids frills and verbal tricks.

Gone are the virtues of polysyllabic words and lumbering sentences. To load a composition with inflated phrases and far-fetched words is now a gross literary vice.

If you would write plainly, beware of affected words and phrases. Do not write *eventuate* when you mean *happen, conversed* for *talked, demise* for *death, a member of the sterner sex* for *man, organ of vision* for *eye, voiced the opinion* for *said*. These are a few examples of tinsel expressions that try to usurp the place of simple words.

Be vigilant! Test every word and phrase to satisfy yourself of its fitness. If you hold to this rule, you will soon learn to distinguish the false from the true.

In their desire to avoid repetition many writers resort to the device known as " elegant variation." If the mayor has been mentioned, he makes further appearance as " the civic chief," " the leader of our municipal life," " our official head," " the town's chief representative "—and so on. Variation of this kind should be employed only when it is absolutely necessary. In most cases it is better to use a pronoun.

If you doubt the power of simplicity—if you think that a big subject demands important-looking words —read and re-read the following noble passage from Abraham Lincoln's speech at the dedication of the national cemetery at Gettysburg during the American Civil War :—

> The brave men, living and dead, who struggled here, have consecrated it far above our power to add or detract. The world will little note nor long remember what we say here, but it can never forget what they did here. It is for us, the living, rather, to be dedicated here to the unfinished work which they who fought here have thus far so nobly advanced. It is rather for us to be here dedicated to the great task remaining before us ; that from these honoured dead we take increased devotion to that cause for which they gave the last full measure of devotion ; that we here highly resolve that these dead shall not have died in vain ; that this nation, under God, shall have a new birth of freedom ; and that government of the people, by the people, and for the people, shall not perish from the earth.

THOSE READY-MADE EXPRESSIONS

BE on your guard against worn-out phrases. Nothing more surely betrays a writer's style than the use of stereotyped expressions. The following are typical :—

(a) General.

A few well-chosen words.
Auspicious occasion.
Better half.
Blushing bride.
Bounden duty.
Conspicuous by their absence.
Devoutly hoped.
Eloquent silence.
Eminently successful.
Hale and hearty.
Highly respected.
Immaculate attire.
It stands to reason.
Left severely alone.
Long-felt want.

Numerous and costly.
Old Sol.
Only too happy to.
Sacred edifice.
Sickening thud.
Sweet seventeen.
Tendered his thanks.
The cup that cheers.
The curate's egg.
The festive board.
The finger of fate.
The flowing bowl.
The nuptial knot.

(b) Commercial.

Acknowledging your favour.
Anticipating your prompt attention.
As per your letter.
Awaiting your esteemed instructions.
Beg to enclose.
Earliest convenience.
Even date.
Hoping for a continuance of past favours.
In reply beg to advise.
In reply would say.
Referring to yours.
Same has received attention.
Thanking you in advance (anticipation).
Trusting to receive your further commands.

We beg to remain.
We beg to say.
We must thank you.
We take pleasure in handing you.
Your esteemed instructions.
Your favour duly received.

ANTIQUATED WORDS

THE following list contains a selection of the many antiquated words to be found in the dictionary. Their modern equivalents are given in parenthesis :—

Albeit	(although).
Anent	(about).
Betwixt	(between).
Ere	(before).
Erstwhile	(former).
Hereof	(of this).
Hereunto	(unto this).
Howbeit	(nevertheless).
Nigh	(near).
Ofttimes	(often).
Peradventure	(perhaps).
Perchance	(perhaps)
Save	(except).
Whereas	(since).
Wherefore	(for which reason).
Whereof	(of which).
Wot	(know).

that you are trying to show what a clever fellow you are.   If your letters or your articles are sprinkled with foreign words or phrases, you will soon weary the reader.   You should never borrow from another language if an English equivalent will meet the need.

Finally, Is it YOU?   Do you say things in your own way, or are you content to repeat the expressions worn threadbare by countless pens?   Don't surrender to the lure of the hackneyed phrase.   Be yourself!

PRACTICAL HANDBOOK SERIES

BY JOHN RIGG

HOW TO TAKE THE CHAIR

Fourth Impression   *Limp Cloth, 2s.*

"A comprehensive guide. The section on amendments will be found particularly lucid and helpful."—*Birmingham Gazette*

HOW TO CONDUCT A MEETING

Seventh Impression   *Limp Cloth, 2s.*

"A useful handy book."—*Star*

WHAT TO LOOK FOR IN A PROSPECTUS
With a Note on Balance Sheets

BY A. EMIL DAVIES

Limp Cloth, 2s.

"A small book, but well worth the money."—*Investor's Review*

A SIMPLE GUIDE TO COMMITTEE PROCEDURE
and the work of the Officers of a Society or Club

BY E. O. LAMBOURN

New Edition, Revised and Enlarged   *Limp Cloth, 2s.*

"With this little book in his hand, no entrant into public life need fear to undertake definite duties for the cause or object in which he is interested."—*Yorkshire Post*

PRACTICAL HANDBOOK SERIES

RADIO DRAMA AND HOW TO WRITE IT
BY GORDON LEA

With a Preface by R. E. JEFFREY, Productions Director of the B.B.C.

Cloth Boards, 3s.   *Limp Cloth*, 2s.

This book, which is the outcome of a large practical experience in the preparation and production of Radio Plays, should inspire writers to work for this new medium, which is shown to have such potentialities.

HOW TO SUCCEED ON THE STAGE
BY P. BEAUFOY BARRY

Preface by SARA ALLGOOD

Limp Cloth, 2s.

Concisely but thoroughly every essential detail is recorded from the first beginning on the stage until ultimate success is achieved.

GRAMMAR FOR GROWN-UPS
BY CHARLES C. BOYD

Cloth Boards, 3s.   *Third Impression*   *Limp Cloth*, 2s.

LUCRATIVE HOBBIES
BY WALTER AND LEONARD TOWNSEND

With Illustrations by the Authors   *Limp Cloth*, 2s.

CAREERS FOR GIRLS
BY ELEANOR PAGE

Limp Cloth, 2s.

PRACTICAL HANDBOOK SERIES

SECRETS OF SUCCESS IN PUBLIC SPEAKING
BY MAX CROMBIE
Second Impression   *Limp Cloth, 2s.*

SECRETS OF PROFITABLE WRITING
BY MAX CROMBIE
Limp Cloth, 2s

GRAMMAR FOR GREAT AND SMALL
BY CHARLES C. BOYD
Cloth Boards, 3s.   *Limp Cloth, 2s.*

FREELANCE JOURNALISM
BY VICTOR HYDE
Limp Cloth, 2s.

HOW TO WRITE GOOD ENGLISH
Some Principles of Style
BY HENRY BETT
Third Impression   *Limp Cloth, 2s.*
"It is very, very good. Clear, accurate, picturesque, and positively exciting. . . . It is impeccably written."—MR. ARNOLD BENNETT in the *Evening Standard*

HOW TO WRITE GOOD LETTERS
BY BERYL HEITLAND
Limp Cloth, 2s.
"Sensible, practical, and to the point."—*Everyman*

ABRIDGED AUCTION AND CONTRACT BRIDGE
BY ADA CAMPBELL KELLEY

GEORGE ALLEN & UNWIN LTD
LONDON: 40 MUSEUM STREET, W.C.1
CAPE TOWN: 73 ST. GEORGE'S STREET
SYDNEY, N.S.W.: WYNYARD SQUARE
AUCKLAND, N.Z.: 41 ALBERT STREET
TORONTO: 91 WELLINGTON STREET, WEST